An illustrated
Thames Sailin

2009 Second
ISBN 978-0-956

C000245236

By Peter and Rita Phillips
who have asserted their rights under the
Copyright, Designs and Patents Act, 1988
to be identified as authors of this work.

Published by Phillips Design
Tollesbury
phillipsdesign@hotmail.co.uk

All photographs Copyright Phillips Design unless otherwise stated

Printed by
Think Ink Ipswich

1

Introduction

Welcome to this, the second edition of *An illustrated guide to Thames Sailing Barges*. If like us, you cannot see one of these lovely vessels without wanting to know more about her then we have written this book for you.

We have set out in simple and, as far as possible, non-technical terms, a brief description of the barges which we feel are most likely to be seen around our coastline. Original and contemporary illustrations accompany most entries .

In each case we have listed, where available;

- Date and place of launch
- Port of registration
- Type of construction
- Length
- Beam
- Kind of rig, bowsprit or staysail
- Present operator and usual base

In this edition we have, for simplicity omitted Tonnage and Draught. The National Historic Ships Certificate number where appropriate has been added however. We also feel that readers will be interested to know which barges took part in the Dunkirk evacuation so this is indicated as applicable.

We have added if possible, any other visible aids to identification together with an outline of the history of the particular barge. Web sites given for individual barges were current and working as of June 2009.

We have moved six barges from the main section of the first edition (*Betula, Beric, Lady Jean, Pudge, Thalatta, Xylonite*), either because they are having long term work carried out or because they are listed as "For Sale" and their future usage is uncertain. *Scone* has been omitted altogether as she is reported to have deteriorated significantly on Benfleet Marshes. *British Empire* at Battlesbridge is excluded as she also seems beyond salvation.

We hope that having read this book you will be encouraged to delve deeper into the subject. The web sites of the Association of Dunkirk Little Ships,The Society for Sailing Barge Research, The National Historic Ships Register and the Thames Sailing Barge Trust are particularly useful as, of course, are those of the individual barge owners.

All of the above sources have been invaluable in the preparation of this work as has the contribution of Roger Newlyn of T.S.B.T for his updates.

We hope you enjoy this publication.

The development of the Thames sailing barge

The Thames sailing barges we see today have been evolving since the Middle Ages and, through their various uses as training vessels, private yachts and corporate hospitality centres, continue to evolve today.

Exactly how this evolution has taken place depends to some extent on which historical sources we use, however, in our opinion, it is hard to better the well researched theories of Hervey Benham in his work, *Down Tops'l* (See Bibliography.)

In The Middle Ages, the forerunners of the Thames barges were, simple flat-bottomed small to medium sized open vessels designed to ply the creeks and estuaries of South East England, probably rigged with a single mast and one large square sail.

Decks were introduced, possibly to make the barges more seaworthy as their trade spread from the inland and estuary waterways to coastal and cross channel work. Other sources have it that such work was carried out in these vessels from the very beginning!

One of the first written records of barges trading is Daniel Defoe's account of cargos of chalk being fetched to Essex to lighten the clay soils in the eighteenth century.

By now evolution was continuing apace, leeboards were fitted for added stability, the bow shape evolved from a flat shovel shape, like a lighter, through a raked bow to the vertical stem of today.

Mizzen masts were fitted to improve handling and bowsprits to give more sail area to the bigger coasting barges.

Of the smaller craft, Essex barges generally found a bowsprit useful while their Kentish counterparts, working smoother waters, found a stays'l rig more convenient on the congested "London River."

The nineteenth century saw barges gradually increased in size, with cargoes of 100 - 200 tons common by 1890. Later in that century came another development when the ships wheel started to replace the tiller. The first barge that we know for certain was launched with this arrangement was the *Anglo Saxon* in 1873 or *Anglo-Norman*, depending on which source you use!

Probably the last example of a barge sailing with a tiller is the *Cygnet*, a small 16 ton barge built in 1881 and still to be seen operated single-handed in these waters in the summer months.

The sail arrangements of barges is a story in itself. The spritsail rig, is seen depicted in contemporary paintings of the Thames going back to the seventeenth century, (and was probably used by many sorts of craft for a long time before). Ketch or "boomie" rigs were perhaps more favoured for open water work.

By the beginning of the twentieth century many ketches (such as *Thalatta*) were changed to spritsail rig as a crew of two could work this whereas a "boomie" required up to six hands.

A "Third Hand" would often help with the cooking and general work on board, frequently a youngster learning his trade. *The Thalatta Diaries* published by Heritage House (publishing) Ltd gives a first rate description of what it is like to be a Third Hand today!

The spritsail barges carried a small mizzen though some, mainly used for more sea going work, found a larger ketch rigged mizzen to be handier. These vessels acquired the inelegant, if understandable appellation "mulie."

In their heyday of the late nineteenth and early twentieth century the barge fleet could be found travelling all around the South and Eastern coasts of Britain and up many of the rivers of Continental Europe.

These barges were trading for a wide range of industries, including bricks, ballast and cement for building. (A barge specialising in carrying such a cargo was known as a "brickie")! One barge could carry enough bricks in one cargo to build two semi detached houses!

Coastal barges carried coal from the North East, with perhaps a return trip laden with a cargo of wheat. Even the sea walls built at that time were constructed from stones transported by the barge fleet!

A flourishing trade grew up taking hay and straw to London to supply the horse drawn transport system, the return journey being made with a cargo of the recycled product to act as manure for the East Anglian farmers!

Barges in this trade were known as "stackies" from the way their cargoes were frequently stacked above deck. Usually built with slightly wider decks, some sported longer sprits to allow the mains'l to be reefed up clear of the stack.

In short, if something needed taking to or from the Capital or from farm to mill, there was a good chance it would go by barge. They were in fact, the H G V's of their day.

It can be said that the growth of the British economy, infrastructure and hence Empire, in the nineteenth and early twentieth centuries depended less on "Ships of the Line" than on the humble Thames sailing barge.

ARDWINA of London

Staysail Class   *Official No. 129016*   *NHSR Cert. No.190*

'Bob' - Red 'A' & navigational dividers on 3 blue horizontal bands on white ground. Has "Rolfe Judd" in topsail.

The last wooden barge built by Orvis and Fuller at Ipswich in 1909. *Ardwina* has lead a chequered existence.

Much of her working life was spent in general trade on the East Coast.

In 1938, having lost her mast, she was abandoned at sea, eventually being recovered by Ocean Salvage.

Subsequently she was engaged in the stone trade from Portland to Greenwich until 1952 and was a houseboat at Chelsea in the 1970's.

Fortunately *Ardwina* has survived all her troubles and based at St. Katharine's is now operated by Ardwina Ltd as a charter and hospitality barge for her owners Rolfe Judd Ltd, a London firm of Architects.

Ardwina regularly participates in Barge Matches around our coast but is seen here having work carried out at Fullbridge in the Autumn of 2008.

Length 85 ft Beam 21.1 ft

ADIEU of Harwich
Bowsprit Class   Official No. 161035

'Bob' - Plain light blue. Green trim to gunwale.

Built of Steel in 1929 by Horlock's for F. W. Horlock & Co Ltd, a sister ship to *Portlight, Xylonite, Reminder and Repertor.*

Converted to a motor barge in 1949 and laid up as a lighter in 1967, she gradually became a rusting hulk like so many of her breed.

Bought by James Stewart in 1985, her "wafer thin" bottom was renewed by James and Stone. Restoration continued until 1993 and included a new lining, mast and rigging, the permanent sheeting of her holds, a new aft deck, the complete replacement of all deck gear (except the main horse) and many other details.

Now owned and operated by Iolo Brooks *Adieu* has the distinction of being one of the last barges to be worked on at the Old Dolphin Yard at Sittingbourne when she had her sails dressed there a few years ago.

Usually based at St Katharine's dock, *Adieu* is a regular competitor in Barge Matches around the coast though not always deploying the fine blue and white sail seen here at the Blackwater Match of 2008.

CABBY of Rochester

Bowsprit Class   Official No. 160687   NHSR Core Collection Cert. No. 134

'Bob' - Plain white C on plain red ground. Dark grey lower hull with black wale.

The last full size barge built of wood at Rochester in 1928 by Gill, for the London & Rochester Barge Company. Work started in 1925 but because of the economic climate at the time she was not completed until three years later.

In 1940, when at Ipswich, she was ordered to Dunkirk with drums of freshwater for the troops. Redirected to Brest, she was finally ordered to Plymouth without reaching France!

Subsequent war service saw her visit Ireland, the Clyde and the Hebrides where she was given a new wheelhouse.

After the war she returned to trade, working as a motor barge, her last cargo trip being made in the late 1960's. She was re-rigged in 1970 and used as a company charter barge.

Since then *Cabby* has had several owners, now being operated by Sailing Barge Cabby Ltd of Maylandsea. The photograph shows her off Stansgate in the summer of 2008.

www.sailingbargecabbyltd.com

Length 91.93 ft Beam 21.5 ft   Dunkirk Little Ship

CENTAUR of Harwich

Staysail Class   Official No. 99460   NHSR Cert. No. 193

'Bob' - Gold wheel on red & black ground.

Built of wood at Harwich in 1895 by John and Herbert Cann, She was originally owned by Charles Stone, but passed through a number of other owners before being bought by Francis & Gilders and later by the London & Rochester Trading Company.

1944 saw her in the service of Brown and Co who had her de-rigged and employed as a timber lighter.

Bought in 1966 by Richard Duke who re-rigged her and used her as a charter barge before selling her in 1974 to the Thames Barge Sailing Club (now Trust) for members sailing.

Based at Maldon and rebuilt 1984-95, *Centaur* is now owned by the Thames Sailing Barge Trust. This is an organisation dedicated to promoting and teaching the practice of the traditional skills of seamanship involved in sailing and maintaining these historic craft.

Here *Centaur* is pictured taking advantage of a stiff breeze as she approaches Mersea Stone at the beginning of June 2009.

www.bargetrust.org   *Length 85.54 ft Beam 19.5 ft*

CYGNET of Harwich
Bowsprit Class   Official No. 84028   NHSR Cert. No.194

'Bob' - Plain red.

A half size working barge she was built of wood in 1881 by Curel for use trading to small farm creeks. Originally owned by Walter Wrinch of Ewarton.

Although half the length of a full size barge she registers only 16 tons which is roughly a quarter of the capacity of such a craft.

Owned by Mica Brown who refitted her as a private yacht based at Snape Maltings, *Cygnet* has her mizzen stepped on her rudder post and has a tiller rather than a wheel for steering.

Regularly sailed single handed by Des Kaliszew. *Cygnet* caused quite a stir recently when sailing the area laden with a stack of straw stowed on her deck in traditional manner. This gave rise to fanciful stories in the local press of "ghost ships" from the past!

Length 41.96 ft   Beam 12.98 ft

DAWN of Maldon
Bowsprit Class   *Official No. 105902*   *NHSR Cert. No. 221*

'Bob'- Plain dark blue. Cream gunwale.

Built of wood in 1897 by Walter Cook of Maldon for James Keeble. A "stackie," she was reckoned to be one of the handiest of the breed, the only one never to lose a stack over the side.

Dawn appears on the register of "Dunkirk Little Ships" though having suffered a collision at Dover, she may not have reached France.

Becoming a motor barge and then a lighter, *Dawn* was rescued by Gordon Swift in 1967 and re-rigged and used as a charter barge from Maldon. 1978 saw her pass to the London Borough of Newham which used her as a sailing school.

After a period of disuse and general deterioration she was rescued by the formation of the "Dawn Sailing Barge Trust." In 1999 *Dawn* was moved from Hoo in Kent, to Maldon and thence to Heybridge in 2002 for restoration with the help of a National Lottery grant.

Work was completed in 2008 when she received a new suit of sails made by North Sea Sails of Tollesbury. *Dawn* is seen here taking part in the Blackwater Barge Match as part of her Sea Trials.

www.dawn-trust.org.uk   *Length 81.9 ft Beam 20 ft Dunkirk Little Ship*

DECIMA of London
Staysail Class   Official No. 110055

'Bob' - 2 dark blue horizontal bands, with black 'G' in gold on central horizontal band. White gunwale.

Built of steel by Fay at Southampton in 1899, for E. J. & W. Goldsmith Ltd. of Grays. She is believed to be the last barge from this builder to still be sailing.

She continued to carry general cargo for this owner until the late 1940's when she was sold to Rayfields at Gravesend. In the 1960's she was converted to a motor barge and went to Greenhithe Lighterage Co Ltd.

Decima was re-rigged as a sailing barge when she left trade in 1977, having been bought by Dennis Wildish who operated her thus for some years. Sold in 1996 she was used as a houseboat on Faversham creek.

Decima's fortunes were to take a turn for the better when she was purchased by Tim Goldsack in 2003 since when she has sailed regularly. Given a new tops'l in 2006 from the *"May"* together with new plating and engines, she is once more in fine shape, as can be seen in this photograph taken from *S B Reminder* in 2007.

Length 85 ft   Beam 19.6 ft

EDME of Harwich
Bowsprit Class   Official No. 105425

'Bob' - White 'H' on red ground. White 'EDME' in topsail.

Built of wood by J & H Cann in 1898 for F. W Horlock. Named after the English Diastatic Malt Extract Company (which continues to operate at Mistley to this day). *Edme* continued in trade under sail until 1949 when she was de-rigged and used as a lighter by Brown and Co.

When her days as a lighter were over, *Edme* underwent a lengthy period of restoration at Maldon before being bought by the Harman-Harrison Consortium in 1989.

In 2002 the EDME company sponsored a new tops'l for *Edme* and commissioned her to carry flour from Mistly Quay to Greens flower Mill in Maldon, the first time a Thames sailing barge had carried such a cargo since the 1970's

Now based at skipper Andy Harman's boat yard at St Osyth, (Where *Thalatta* is undergoing her refit), she is used for charter work out of Brightlingsea having a sailing capacity of twelve passengers.

Edme still operates under sail only, not having an engine. She continues to enjoy a successful career as a racing barge.

Length 80 ft   Beam 17.25 ft

FERTILE
Bowsprit Class   SSR No 65378

'Bob' - Brown eagle with yellow barge on dark blue ground.

Built as a Thames lighter in 1935, she was found in a Medway scrap yard in 1984 and converted to a sailing barge.With her "stumpy" rig and "swim head" bow she provides a unique glimpse of an earlier era of barging.

Owned and operated by Fertile-Charters of Colchester, who use her for regular musical excursions and for chartering. She is seen here at King Edward Quay, Colchester in January 2009.

Swim head bow

www.fertile-charters.co.uk   *Length 72 ft Beam 18 ft*

GLADYS of Harwich

'Bob' - Green, orange & gold triangular. 'Kingsmill' emblem in topsail

Built by Cann of Harwich, of wood in 1901. *Gladys's* first owners were William Thomas Whitmore, of Harwich (master mariner with 48 shares) and John Howard (master mariner with 16 shares) of Shoeburyness. She was sold to John Lesley Whitemore of Lancashire a year later though John Howard remained as master.

Gladys was sold to Cranfield Brothers Ltd, with Charles Howard as the master in 1912. In 1950 a diesel engine was fitted and she was re registered.

Passing to Mardorf Peach Ltd in the early 1970's she was re-rigged and served as a company yacht.

Gladys was acquired by her present owners, Allied Mills in 1999 and fitted with a new transom in 2003.

Gladys continues as a company yacht based at St. Katharine's Dock, she is pictured making her way to the Pin Mill Barge Match in 2008.

Gladys spent the winter of 2008/9 at Heybridge Basin.

Length 84 ft Beam 20.6 ft

GRETA of Colchester
Staysail Class   *Official No. 98324*

Photo courtesy Steve Norris

Bob- Red N on black &gold ground. Topsail has white Shepherds crook and mainsail has white 'SHEPHERD NEAME, BREWER, FAVERSHAM

Built of wood by Stone of Brightlingsea in 1892 for a Sailmaker named Hibbs. In his book "Barges" (Adlard Coles, l984) John Leather maintains that Hibbs perfected the process, using a dressing including horse fat, which gave sails their resistance to hard wear, and traditional colour. Later, oil and red ochre were also used.

Greta passed from Hibbs to the fleet of Owen Parry where she usually carried such cargo as grain and malt. A notable exception was when she carried the spars for the Kaisers racing schooner! *Greta* was sold to the London Rochester Barge Company in 1918. Passing out of trade in the 1960's *Greta* was converted to a houseboat and re rigged, having become a motor barge in 1951.

Greta is said to be the oldest active barge to have taken part in the Dunkirk evacuation and took part in the 60th anniversary celebrations, Prince Charles coming aboard to speak with Skipper/Owner Steve Norris.

In 2008 a grant was received from National Historic Ships for replacement of the fore and aft main hatches. Based at Faversham, *Greta* is available for charter and still takes part in Barge Matches.

www.greta1892.co.uk   *Length 80ft Beam 20 ft*   *Dunkirk Little Ship*

HYDROGEN of London

Bowsprit Class   *Official No. 123640*   *NHSR Cert. No. 208*

'Bob' - Green, red & white

Built of wood in 1906 by Gills of Rochester to carry tar and oil, she had her tanks for these removed in 1910 when she was sold to G Andrews who used her for general cargo work.

During this time she would carry cement up to the Humber, returning to the Thames and Medway rivers with coal.

Ownership having passed to G F Sully, she was commandeered in 1941 and did her war service on the Clyde. After the war she returned to trade, operating until 1976 though as a motor rather than sailing barge.

Hydrogen was purchased by Bells whisky in 1978 for whom she became a well known sight round the UK coast, entertaining many of her owners guests in ports en-route. For this work she was returned to sail as a "mulie," reputedly having the tallest mizzen in the fleet!

Bought by the Blackwater Barge Co in 1992, *Hydrogen* now operates as a charter barge out of Maldon for Topsail Charters, as such she is the largest wooden barge still sailing.

Length 94.75 ft Beam 24.49 ft

KITTY of Harwich

'Bob' - White star on red ground. White star in topsail. Green hull.

Built of wood in 1895 by J.H.Cann of Harwich for Horlocks as part of their fleet of grain carriers. In WW1 *Kitty* carried out the dangerous task of transporting stores across the channel to Calais and Boulogne.

Francis & Gilders bought *Kitty* in 1938 later passing her on to the London and Rochester Trading Company who continued to employ her in trade until selling her on to Brown and Co who used her as a timber lighter.

1964/5 saw *Kitty's* prospects improve when she was bought by Maldon Yacht and Barge Charter Ltd and re-rigged as a charter vessel.

Becoming a notable racing barge *Kitty* eventually changed owners and went to Port Solent for use as a Corporate Entertainment barge under private owner-ship.

Put up for sale in 2008, *Kitty* is currently operated by Topsail Charters of Maldon, receiving a licence for the sale of alcohol and for musical entertainment from Maldon District Council in March 2009. She is a colourful addition to the Blackwater charter community.

Length 82.13ft Beam 19.38ft

LADY DAPHNE of Rochester
Staysail Class   Official No. 127276

'Bob' - blue and red .White Z in topsail   Photo courtesy William Joseph

Built of wood in 1923 by Short Bros. of Rochester for David J Bradley for whose family she continued to trade until joining the fleet of R & W Paul (Maltsters) Ltd of Ipswich in 1937.

Having been first fitted with an engine in 1932 *Lady Daphne* was re-engined with a Ruston and Hornsby 5 cylinder motor in 1947. Some ten years later sail gave way to power completely and she operated as a motor barge until sold to Taylor Woodrow Property Ltd in 1973.

New owners meant a new lease of life under sail as *Lady Daphne* was re rigged and used as a charter and promotional vessel.

In 1996 ownership passed to Elisabeth and Michael Mainelli who operate her as managing agents under the banner of Nymph Ltd. Topsail Events and Char-ters frequently using *Lady Daphne* for charters based at St. Katharine's Dock.

Lady Daphne has recently been an occasional Barge Match competitor.

Listed as "For sale" in April 2009, Topsail Events continue to use her.

www.lady-daphne.co.uk   *Length 90.8 ft Beam 21.4 ft*

LADY OF THE LEA of Dover
Staysail Class   Official No. 722956

Bob' - plain red. Has white barge inside castle, all inside double circle emblem in topsail

Built of wood in 1931 by Hyam & Oliver at Rotherhithe as a "War Department Sailing Barge", her early duties were to carry armaments between Waltham Abbey and Woolwich Arsenal.

Lady of the Lea was the last sailing barge to be built following the plans of canal barges from a century earlier and originally had tiller steering and was stumpy rigged. To deal with her part open river and part canal journeys she was often powered by horse as well as sail!

A petrol engine was added by the Navy in 1943, this was replaced by a diesel in 1980. She was sold to W Aslett in 1946 and subsequently to her present owner Brian Pain. She was largely rebuilt between 1980 and 1990 including doubling the bottom and lower hull.

Based at Faversham *Lady of the Lea* is a regular Barge Match competitor and is photographed here during the Medway Barge Match of 2009.

Length 72 ft Beam 13 ft

MARJORIE of Ipswich
Bowsprit Class   Official No. 113753

'Bob' - Lemon & black quarters with lemon 'D' & '105' on black quarters

Owned initially by R & W Paul Ltd and sailing as a coastal barge she continued to trade under sail until 1961 when she became a charter barge owned by Mr A.J.O'Shea and based at Maldon.

Marjorie continued at Maldon for some time and still visits for the Blackwater Barge Match.

After a period of ownership by Albert Groom, she passed to barrister Simon Devonshire who had her restored by Robert Deards who also skippers her.

Based in Robert's yard at Hoo or at St Katherine's Dock in London, *Marjorie* sadly suffered collision damage in the Swale Barge Match of 2008 which put her out of action for some months.

Happily at the time of writing repair work is almost complete and it is expected that she will be sailing before the end of the 2009 summer.

With her varnished transom and dark grey hull *Marjorie* is one of the prettiest barges around.

Length 84 ft Beam 19.3 ft

MIROSA of Maldon

Bowsprit Class   *Official No. 96488   NHSR Core Collection. Cert. No. 215*

'Bob' - Lemon Tudor rose on blue ground.

Built as the stack barge *Ready* at Maldon in 1892 by John Howard. Originally owned by Charles Gutteridge of Vauxhall and later by W. W. Keeble, she was renamed *Mirosa* in 1947.

One of the last barges to earn her living entirely under sail, she has never had an engine fitted.

Mirosa continued in trade until 1955 when she was used as a timber lighter until being restored with a full set of traditional flax sails and manila (as opposed to steel) rigging by new, private owners in 1965. She is now owned by Peter Dodds and based at Iron Wharf, Favesham.

Mirosa still has no motor and can be seen from time to time being towed up river by a local tug, a sight evocative of earlier times.

A highly successful racing barge, *Mirosa* is pictured approaching the start of the Medway Match in 2009.

Length 82 ft Beam 20.75 ft

NELLIE of Faversham

Staysail Class *Official No. 114452*

'Bob' - Plain emerald green

Built of wood at Faversham for Charles Cremer, the brick manufacturer in 1901. *Nellie* was used mainly for river work for most of her life, no doubt transporting many of the ten million bricks a year turned out by that firm. Certainly she was still working for Cremer's in 1938 according to the Merchant Navy List.

Nellie was bought by R Lapthorn & Co Ltd. In 1951 for whom she worked until 1960. When Tony Lapthorn and his Son retired a few years ago the Company was sold to new owners who traded as Coastal Bulk Shipping Ltd.(Which sadly ceased trading at the end of 2008). *Nellie* was operated as a motor barge from 1952.

Coming out of trade, *Nellie* was used for years as a houseboat, before being rebuilt at Twickenham in 1985 and completed by Cooks of Maldon in 1994. *Nellie* is now owned by Professor Diane Montgomery, who uses her as a floating home.

Nellie is unusual in that she is "stumpy" rigged with no topmast, as can be clearly seen in this picture taken when she attended the Blackwater Barge Match of 2008.

ORINOCO of London
Staysail Class   Official No.104862

'Bob' - plain dark green

Built of wood by Hughes at East Greenwich in 1895 and said to be the last remaining active barge from that area. Originally owned by Masons the cement makers, *Orinoco* passed to Cranfield Bros, possibly when Masons ceased trading in 1907. In any case, *Orinoco* was listed as Cranfield's in the 1916 Merchant Navy List.

During a long career with Cranfield's she had a Ruston Auxiliary engine fitted. Retirement came eventually however and by the 1970's she had been sold to and re-fitted by a private owner.

In 1990, *Orinoco* was fitted out as a private yacht barge at Hoo where part owner Robert Deards skippered her in races.

Now owned by Geoffrey Ingle *Orinoco* is based at Faversham and continues to compete in local Barge Matches. She is pictured here attending the Medway Match in May 2009.

PHOENICIAN of London

'Bob' - Blue, gold, red & white

Built of wood by Wills and Packham at Sittingbourne in 1922 and believed to be the last wooden Thames barge built. *Phoenician's* early owners included E. A. Horlock and R. Sulley.

Said to have been built partly for racing, she was a very successful competitor in pre war Barge Matches.

During World War Two, *Phoenician* survived an aircraft crash landing on her and thereafter went to the Walton Backwaters mooring barrage balloons. Re-built at government expense, she was converted to a motor barge.

Sold out of trade to Albert Groom in 1949 and used for chartering and "community" purposes she moved to several bases before being restored and re-rigged at Maldon in 1998.

Phoenician is now owned by Grant Littler and based at St. Katharine's. She is pictured taking advantage of a brisk breeze as she heads for the finish of the Medway Barge Match of 2009.

Length 79.93 ft   Beam 20 ft

REMINDER of Harwich

Staysail Class   *Official No. 161033*

'Bob' - Green, red & white. White hull.

Built of steel at Mistley in 1929 by Horlock and owned by Fred Horlock.

According to tradition, she gained her name from a promise made by Fred Horlock after the 1928 Thames Barge Match, that he would "Remind" his rivals of the speed of his barges. The many successes enjoyed in Thames and Medway Matches since would suggest that this was no idle boast.

Reminder spent much of her working life transporting acid from London to the British Xylonite Plastics Ltd factory at Manningtree as well as the family trade of carrying malt and barley.

She continued to carry cargoes under sail until an engine was installed in 1947.

Once her career in trade was over, *Reminder* was re-rigged as a charter barge by Roger Beckett of Anglian Yacht Services for chartering out of Maldon.

Owned by Reminder (1929) Ltd and managed by Topsail Charters. *Reminder* is still based at Maldon and seen here at Pin Mill.

Length 87.83 ft Beam 19.38 ft

REPERTOR of Harwich

Staysail Class   *Official No. 145404*

'Bob' - White fish (Pollock) emblem with black 'P' on red ground. Red gunwale

Built of steel at Mistley in 1924 by Horlock for owners M.R.Horlock.

The name "*Repertor*" means, in Latin, discoverer, explorer, inventor, innovator or deviser.

After a long career in trade, both as a sailing barge and a motor tanker barge, she was sold out of trade to G. Reeve and served for a time as a houseboat at Battersea.

Repertor was re-rigged by C.McLaren in 1987 and is now owned by David Pollack.

Although usually based at Standard Quay, Faversham she is also to be seen in the Maldon area as she is chartered through Topsail Charters of Hythe Quay.

A keen Barge Match competitor she is pictured above at the 2008 Blackwater Match.

Length 86 ft Beam 20 ft

THISTLE of London

Bowsprit Class   *Official No. 105727*   *NHSR Cert. No. 188*

'Bob' in 2004 - Green, red & white. Grey gunwale.

Built at Port Glasgow in 1895 by William Hamilton and Sons, she is the oldest surviving Iron sailing barge and the only one built in Scotland to still be sailing.

Thistle spent her early life trading for a London coal merchant before being sold to The London & Rochester Trading Co in the 1920's.

Her first engine was fitted in 1948 and she now operates with a Gardner diesel which was installed in 1980.

She continued to trade in the Thames Estuary until the 1970's.

Thistle went through a number of private owners, being completely restored in the 1980's before passing to *Thistle* (1895) Ltd and operated by Topsail Charters of Maldon.

When operating as a charter barge, she has a sailing capacity of 50 passengers, Her usual charter areas are the East Coast and London, *Thistle* is seen here on a charter to view the Blackwater Barge Match in 2008.

Length 85.93 ft Beam 22 ft

VICTOR of London

Staysail Class   Official No. 105762   NHSR Cert. No. 232

'Bob' - White V and 1895 on dark green ground

Built of wood at the Dock End yard, Ipswich in 1895 by Shrubsall for owner Owen Parry. She carried linseed from East Coast farms to Parry's Mill in Colchester, then took the processed oil in drums to London. When Parry was bought out by the London and Rochester Trading Co in 1932, Victor was valued at £450.

Victor saw war service at Chatham carrying munitions. She escaped a near miss when the lighter next to her received a direct hit from a bomb. She survived to resume her service with L.R.T.C. becoming a motor barge in 1947.

Victor was sold in 1964 again for £450! Subsequently, she had a varied career including being a strip club and houseboat until she was purchased and re-rigged in 1974 by Owen Emerson. Victor was sold to Nick Briggs in 1995 and used for charter work on the Solent.

Having undergone a major refit in 2005/6 Victor is now operated as a charter barge by Classic Yacht Charter Ltd and based at Mistley.

www.sbvictor.co.uk   Length 83.6 ft Beam 20.30 ft

WHIPPET
Staysail Class

'Bob' - Blue with white emblem

Whippet was built and worked for Humphrey and Gray mainly in the Pool of London. She was employed as a bonded barge, which in itself makes her an extremely rare vessel.

A bonded barge is one that loads its cargo, the hold is then locked and a customs seal attached. The seal remains until the goods are either:-
1. Exported 2. Landed and the duty paid 3. Stored in a Bonded Warehouse under a similar custom's seal.

Whippet was never 'towed' but was 'rowed' or 'driven' with sweeps (oars) by a licensed waterman.

Purchased by Reggie Coombes in 1969, she was maintained in working condition. later being rigged as a sailing barge and operated until the mid 1980's as, "The only iron, swim headed, lug mizzen, gaff rigged, tiller steered, topsail rigged sailing barge in the world - without an engine."

Purchased by Owen and Rita Emerson, *Whippet* has been re-commissioned with a new, conventional bow and stern fitted. Pictured at the Barge Match of her native Medway in 2009.

30

WILL of Maldon.

Staysail Class   *Official No. 148677*   *NHSR Cert No.234*

Photo, courtesy Topsail Events and Charters

Bob' - white tower emblem on dark blue ground.

One of four barges built of steel by Fellows Ltd of Yarmouth for F. T. Everard & Co Ltd as the *Will Everard*. Each barge bore the name of one of the partners in the family firm (Alf, Ethel, Fred and Will). These are said to have been the largest spritsail barges ever built.

The *Will Everard* served the firm for forty years plying her trade round the East and South coasts, acquiring an auxiliary engine in 1951. Everards eventually sold the barge to a private owner in 1966 for the sum of £750 (£250 more than her original price!). A condition of sale was her name could not be retained.

Under her new name of *Will* and now registered at Maldon, the barge languished on the Blackwater for two years before being resold to John Hubbins who re rigged her and installed a new engine.

After two years as a barge yacht *Will* was sold to O.C.L Ltd (Later P & O) who refitted her for corporate entertainment and promotional work. *Will* was Sold in 1998 to Skipper Sue Harrison who in turn sold her to a private owner in 2004.

Will is now operated by Topsail Events and Charters of Brighton and works mainly from St. Katharine's Dock.

Length 97.54 ft Beam 24.54 ft

WYVENHOE of London

Staysail Class   *Official No. 110012*   *NHSR Cert. No. 235*

'Bob' - Red & white horizontal bands. Dark grey gunwale.

Built of steel at Wivenhoe by Forrestt & Sons Ltd in 1898, for a London owner specifically for entering Barge Matches. She was sold to the London & Rochester Trading Co and began her life as a commercial barge in 1903.

In 1923 she was fitted with her first engine and her rigging removed. Continuing in trade until 1983, *Wyvenhoe* is claimed to hold the record for the longest working life of any British registered vessel in this country.

Wyvenhoe was purchased and re-rigged as a company yacht barge by R.Walsh, of Wyvenhoe (London) Ltd. She was bought by Martin Phillips in 2004.

Having once featured in the Bond film "The world is not enough", *Wyvenhoe* now operates as a charter barge, based at Maldon, licensed to carry twelve passengers.

In 2008 she was used on several school trips and for charter to The Medway, Pin Mill and Blackwater Barge Matches.

Wyvenhoe is captured here off Mersea Stone in June 2009.

www.wyvenhoe.co.uk   *Length 83.93 ft Beam 18.89 ft*

LUCTOR ET EMERGO
Dutch barge

Not strictly within the scope of this booklet but we hope, of interest, are a small number of Dutch barges which are seen from time to time around the East Coast.

With a working history in many ways similar to our own barges, they share many of their characteristics, such as flat bottoms, lee boards and shallow draught.

In appearance Dutch tjalk barges usually have a slightly more rounded look to the hull (tjalk can be translated as 'like a rounded box') and most seen today have a single mast with a large boom.

Historically, Dutch barges have carried as diverse rigs as our own, with the familiar Sprits'l arrangement common many years ago.

The *Luctor Et Emergo* pictured above. Is an occasional visitor to the Blackwater Estuary sometimes to be seen tied up at Maldon Quay side.

She is a sea going tjalk barge, owned by Guus Dral, one of Holland's leading Bassoonists and son of Cor Dral, the well known Amsterdam artist of the 1990's.

And Also...
The following are believed to be actually or potentially "Active."

ALICE of Rochester. *Staysail Class. 'Bob' - blue G on yellow ground*
Built 1954 as Swim Head Lighter. Converted 1997. SSR No 68024. Operated on the South coast by Alice 4 Charter.

ATRATO of London. *Staysail Class. 'Bob' - 2 lemon diamonds on black ground*
Official No. 110037. Built 1898 of steel. Owner Rupert Ashmore. Based Battersea.

BERIC of Harwich. *Staysail Class. 'Bob' Dark blue & white with white P in green disc on white half.*
Official No 105421. Built of wood at Harwich 1896. For sale as a houseboat, June 2009.

BETULA of Ipswich. *Staysail Class. 'Bob' Plain red. Cream trim on Gunwale*
Originally built in Holland as a bulk cement carrier *Maartelaasgracht*. Converted 1997. Based Pin mill from where she may continue to operate. For sale June 2009.

ENA of Ipswich. *Staysail Class. 'Bob' - white cross on red ground. White cross in topsail.*
Official No. 122974. Built of wood at Harwich in 1906. Based Hoo, Kent. Major refit 2001 featured on TV programme "Salvage Squad." Believed inactive following a serious injury to her owner. Dunkirk Little Ship.

ETHEL ADA of London. *Staysail Class. 'Bob' - red & blue horizontal bands with 2 white vertical bars.*
Official No.118352. Built of wood in 1903 Owner, Oliver Price, Based St. Katharine's.

HENRY of London. *Staysail Class. 'Bob' - swallowtail with white central horizontal band on dark blue ground. Green transom.*
Official No. 118381. Built of wood at Goldsmiths yard Grays in 1904. Underwent a major re fit in 2003. Owned Justin Ford, based at Faversham.

LADY JEAN of Rochester. *Staysail Class. 'Bob' White 'W' on red ground*
Official No.148366. Built of wood by Short Bros. Of Rochester in 1926. Changed owners and undergoing extensive work.

MAY of Ipswich. *Bowsprit Class. 'Bob' - blue & white horizontal stripes. White 'TATE & LYLE' in topsail.*
Official No. 97680. Built of wood at Harwich in 1891 Owned Silvertown Services Ltd (Tate & Lyle). Based St. Katharine's. Static for 2009?

MELISSA of London. *Staysail Class.*
Official No.110078. Built of steel at Southampton 1899. Privately owned. Restoration continues and appears near to completion at Pin Mill.

MONTREAL of London. *Staysail Class. 'Bob' - light blue 'M' on black ground.* Official No. 15879, Built Sittingbourne,1902 as swim head lighter.. House boat for some time. Underway again in 2002 and now based at Hoo in Kent.

PUDGE of Rochester. *Staysail Class. 'Bob' Gold wheel emblem on red & black ground.* Official No. 127274 Built 1922 by London and Rochester Trading Co. Owned Thames sailing Barge Trust. Undergoing extensive work 2009. Dunkirk Little ship.

RAYBEL of London. *Staysail Class. 'Bob' in 2004 - white 'H' on dark blue ground.* Official No. 145058, Built of wood at Sittingbourne 1920 Charter barge 2008. Based St. Katharine's.

XYLONITE of Harwich. *Bowsprit Class. 'Bob' White stars & tree emblem on dark blue ground. Avocet design and Suffolk Life in topsail. Distinctive light grey hull.* Official No. 145408 Built of steel at Mistley in 1926 by F W Horlock. Currently in private hands at Mayland having conversion work carried out, she may well be seen again in 2009.

Other barges substantially intact or under restoration.

Cambria	Faversham for restoration.
Edith May	Halstow, undergoing restoration.
Ethel Maud	Medway for restoration.
Felix	At Hoo for refitting.
George Smeed	At Maldon, undergoing re-rigging.
Glenway	Now at Maylandsea, privately owned. Dunkirk Little Ship.
Ironsides	Undergoing refit at Standard Quay Faversham.
Niagara	Hoo for restoration.
Northdown	On exhibition at le Port Musee, Duarnenez, France.
Portlight	Maldon for major refit.
Seagull II	At Gillingham for restoration.
Thalatta	Major rebuild continues at St. Osyth. Now due back in service 2011.
Tollesbury	Barking Creek. For sale. Dunkirk Little Ship.
Vigilant	Private barge yacht, St Osyth.
Violet	Brambletree Wharf, by the New Medway Bridge.
Westmorland	Rebuilding at Faversham.
Wilfred	A night club at Victoria Embankment, near Waterloo Bridge.

Visit www.sailingbargeresearch.org.uk for information on these barges

Bibliography
Web sites

www.adls.org.uk
Association of Dunkirk Little ships web site.
www.bargetrust.org
Charity Dedicated to the Preservation and Sailing of Thames Barges.
www.nationalhistoricships.org.uk
National Historic Ships register. If it's historic and registered, it's there.
www.nmm.ac.uk
The home page of the National Maritime Museum. Picture reference PAF1958 shows an excellent watercolour of Swimheaded barge of the 19th century.
www.sailingbargeassociation.co.uk
For information and news. Has a very readable, if brief, history.
www.sailingbargeresearch.org.uk
Home page of the Society for Sailing Barge Research. Ideal site for the serious student.
www.thalatta.org.uk
Home page of the East Coast Sail Trust and the Thalatta.
www.thamesbarge.org.uk
Thames sailing barge web site, History and news.
www.thamesmatch.co.uk
Thames Sailing Barge Match official web site.
www.topchart.co.uk
Homepage of Topsail Events of Brighton. For private or corporate hire of historic craft.
www.top-sail.co.uk
Topsail Charters. Based at Maldon. For private or corporate hire of sailing barges

Books

The Society for Sailing Barge Research web site has an excellent Bibliography page. (For details contact Roger Newlyn at rogernewlyn@aol.com)
We particularly recommend the following books:

Down Tops'l Published by Harrap,1971. ISBN 0245506616, 9780245506611
Hervey Benham
Sailing Craft of East Anglia Terence Dalton. 1987
Roger Finch & Hervey Benham
Mistleyman's Log (226pp) Fisher Nautical Press. 1977.ISBN 0.904340.01.5
Horlock, A.H. & R.J.
The Thalatta Diaries Heritage House Ltd. ISBN1.85215.1811
Rita Phillips
Coasting Barge Master Edward Arnold Co. 1949 Terence Dalton 1984
Last of the Sailormen Reprint Seafarer Books 1986. ISBN 0.7100.2024.2
 Bob Roberts
The Racing Horlocks 1968-1971 availble from SSBR
Ron Weyda with Bob Horlock